Stepping Back in Time

by Barbara Burt

illustrated by Dick Smolinski

HOUGHTON MIFFLIN BOSTON

The Daydreamer

Katie Smith stared out of her classroom window at the glorious Virginia spring unfolding outside. But her eyes weren't focused on the lush green grass or the tiny leaves opening on all the trees and shrubs. Instead, her mind was filled with thoughts of colonial Williamsburg.

Katie had been volunteering at Williamsburg on weekends for almost a year. Now she wondered what was going on there at that moment. What spring chores were her fellow workers doing? Katie pictured her friends at their work, just as if it were 1775: tending the sheep, churning the butter, preparing the gardens for planting.

Suddenly, a voice interrupted Katie's reverie.

"Earth to Katie, Earth to Katie!" David Jackson, the boy next to her was saying. Startled, Katie remembered where she was. Mr. Berk was writing equations on the blackboard.

"Katie, do you want to come up here and write the answer?" Mr. Berk held out his piece of chalk.

Right, math class, Katie thought to herself. Utterly embarrassed in front of her classmates, Katie wanted to sink into the floor and disappear.

The bell rang. *Saved again!* thought Katie, relieved. As she gathered her books and headed towards the door, Mr. Berk shook his head at her. "Try to pay more attention, you daydreamer."

Katie walked down the hallway, wondering how much algebra she had missed.

It wasn't that Katie hated school. Most of the time she liked it. Her favorite class was history. In fact, it was her history teacher, Miss Rosenberg, who was letting her do a special project on colonial Williamsburg.

When Katie was seven years old, her family had moved from California to Virginia. Katie had been furious with her parents for moving her away from her old school and her friends. But when her parents took her to Williamsburg, which was just a half-hour's drive from their new house, Katie forgave her parents and began to miss California a little less.

Williamsburg had once been the colonial capital of Virginia, and through the centuries people had been preserving it. The town center looked much the same today as it did before the American Revolution. Williamsburg was a place where the democratic ideals of the United States were born, and where Americans fought for their independence from British colonial rule.

To Katie, Williamsburg was a place full of wonder. She loved the feeling of going back in time and discovering what life was like before television and cars and soccer balls. *I was born in the wrong era*, she often thought to herself. *Back then, life was simpler, and girls got to wear pretty dresses. Not only that, but it was a lot easier to daydream while churning butter than it was sitting in math class!* Sometimes Katie even wished she really could step back in time.

From Present to Past

Saturday finally arrived. By now, Saturday mornings had become a special ritual for Katie. It began with her dressing in her colonial outfit. She stepped into her petticoat, the skirt worn beneath her gown. Then came the gown, made of pale green satin, with ruffles on the sleeves and neckline. Next, Katie fastened her hair in a low bun, and pinned her cotton cap onto her head. Women wore caps in colonial Williamsburg to keep dust and dirt out of their hair as well as to avoid spending much time doing up their hair.

After she dressed, Katie rehearsed the lines she would tell visitors when they asked about her work. Playing the role of a young colonial girl was like stepping into a completely different world. The slow rhythms of the work there soothed Katie after a stressful week of school and soccer tournaments.

When she got to Williamsburg, Katie signed in at the main office and headed towards the Geddy House, where she was assigned for the morning. The Geddy House had been built in 1762 by James Geddy, Jr., a gunsmith and brass founder. The cozy yellow house was built in an L-shape, which was unusual for the 18th century. Its design showed ideas that architects used in colonial times. Katie impressed her friends by telling them that the building had "Greek and Roman motifs in a French and Italian style." Not everything, she explained, was built in the English Georgian style back then.

On her way to the Geddy House, Katie walked through the town square with David Jackson from her class. He was dressed in leather shoes, blue stockings, red knickers, a white shirt, and a long tightly fitted brown jacket. It was David's first day on the job.

"You'll love working here, David!" exclaimed Katie. "It's my favorite part of the week."

Katie and David passed the historic capitol building in the town square, from which the British had asserted the King of England's authority over the colonists. Katie thought about all the history the building had seen. Faced with this proud symbol of British rule, many colonists realized that they didn't need a King to rule over them. They were fully capable of writing their own laws and governing themselves in their own way. The town square became a center of debate between the "Crown Loyalists," those in support of British rule, and the "Revolutionaries," who wanted to create a free and independent nation. Eventually, the words between Revolutionaries and Loyalists grew so heated that they led to action, and the Revolutionary War began.

The scent of baking gingerbread escaped from the open door of the Raleigh Tavern Bakery as Katie and David hurried past. As she turned toward the Geddy House, Katie waved goodbye to David, who had to walk farther to reach his assignment.

"Have a great day!" yelled Katie. David waved back and hurried on.

Mrs. Atherton raised her eyebrows as Katie arrived out of breath at the back door of the Geddy House.

"Running a little late, Katie?" she asked.

"Literally!" Katie answered, between gasps.

"Hmm." Mrs. Atherton looked Katie over with a critical eye. "You have picked up a smudge on the back of your gown, but I dare say the visitors won't notice it." Mrs. Atherton told Katie that Daisy Johnson was sitting on the bench out on the front porch, doing her needlework. Katie played soccer with Daisy at school, and was glad to be paired up with her today.

Chores

Daisy, dressed in an outfit much like Katie's, was already at work on her embroidery. Sitting down on the sunny porch, Katie longed for her sunglasses, but she knew that she could not wear them as she worked. There were no sunglasses in historic Williamsburg. She and Daisy exchanged a smile. Their petticoats and gowns were a bit stifling in the steamy weather.

Katie wanted to chat with Daisy, but there were two young visitors standing nearby, watching the girls as they poked their needles in and out through cream-colored muslin. Behind the needles trailed lines of bright embroidery thread. The girls had to stay in character, so talk of school and sports would have to wait until the tourists left.

Just then, David came around the corner of the Geddy House and hurried along the road in front. Forgetting her role for a moment, Katie called out a quick greeting. David began to glance up toward her. But before he looked in her direction, he turned his gaze back down to the road and hurried on without a word. Before Katie knew it, David was turning another corner and disappearing from view.

That's odd, thought Katie, staring after him. Of course she shouldn't have forgotten her role and spoken to David. But it was unlike him to rush on without acknowledging her in some way, even with a smile.

When he passed Katie, David was in the midst of running errands and doing chores. First, he had to bring logs into the house and help start the fires in the main rooms. Finally, he raced to the apothecary to get some herbal medicine. Then he had to help clean the rooms at the inn and prepare them for guests who were arriving later that day. David had only been at his job for two hours and already he was feeling weary.

Meanwhile, Mrs. Atherton called the girls back to the house and set Katie to shucking the corn that was piled by the fireplace. Sitting on the hard wooden chair made Katie's back ache, but she worked in silence.

Daisy was asked to play board games with two other young volunteers. The other jobs performed by the volunteers at the Geddy House were practicing letters on slate boards, completing puzzles, reading 18th-century children's books, rolling hoops, walking on stilts, or playing a game of ninepins. But the young women were usually asked to sew or cook.

Several large groups of tourists trooped through the kitchen but ignored Katie, focusing instead on the board game that Daisy and the others were having so much fun playing. Katie began to daydream as she finished the corn and began to peel potatoes with a short knife. Suddenly, a voice broke through her reverie and Katie looked up. David was standing there, frowning.

"I am here for the butter," David muttered, looking down at his shoes and not at her. Katie handed him a bowl of butter, trying to meet his eyes. She wondered again why David did not talk to her. Just as she was about to ask him, Mrs. Atherton came into the kitchen and sent David on his way immediately. Since there were tourists coming through, Katie couldn't stop David to ask if anything was wrong.

From Past to Present

When Katie finished the kitchen chores, Mrs. Atherton gave her a huge slice of freshly baked bread, slathered with freshly churned butter. After she finished her bread, she sipped a mug of cold apple cider that had been pressed from apples picked at the nearby orchard. The cider was slightly sour, but Katie had gotten used to it. Sugar was expensive in the late 1700s.

Katie's favorite colonial foods were Welsh rabbit, peanut soup, Pennsylvania Dutch apple dumplings, and shepherd's pie, a dish made of boiled potatoes over lamb stew. She loved knowing that the foods were natural, and that the ingredients came from the gardens and farms in and around Williamsburg.

Daisy called for Katie to help set the table. When the sun began to set, their day would finally be over.

When they were done, Katie and Daisy stepped outside. Katie saw David again, this time walking towards Mr. Wetherburn's. But before Katie could call to him, a group of tourists sauntered over to ask her some questions.

"See that boy?" A man pointed to David, who was passing by on the road, running another errand. "Just now, I tried to ask him how to get to the parking lot, but he didn't reply and just looked at the ground. Does he work here?"

"He's playing the part of Rippon, a slave boy who belongs to Mr. Wetherburn," another lady explained. "Does that mean that he can't talk to you either?"

Katie turned to the lady. "A slave boy probably wouldn't be able to talk to us if he didn't know us," she said quietly.

Suddenly Katie knew why David had not responded to her all day. He hadn't been ignoring her. He'd simply been acting as his character should have. Now she remembered that he had mentioned acting the part of an enslaved person at colonial Williamsburg and how the idea had seemed so distant and unreal.

David had said that he wanted to honor his ancestors by showing their role in colonial times, and Katie had agreed that it was a good idea. In the 18th century, half of Williamsburg's population was African American. But Katie hadn't realized how separate their worlds would be.

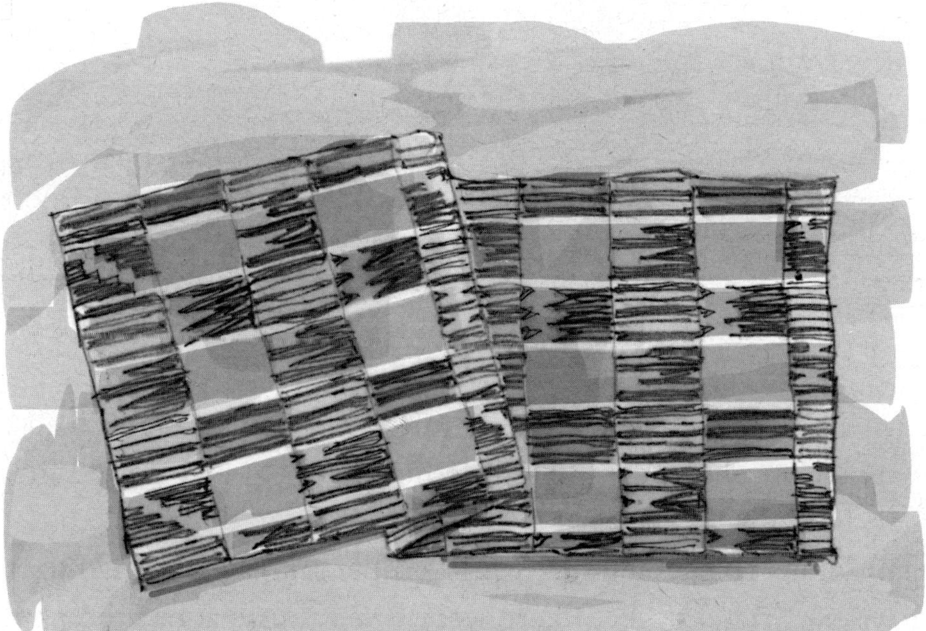

The day ended, and Katie waited for David. He walked over to her and smiled. He told her that he'd had a good first day, but he added that he wasn't quite prepared for how painful his role would be. Katie simply said she was glad to have her friend back. There were some things about the past, Katie realized, that she didn't like at all.